HS AC
HOMELAND SECURITY
OPERATIONAL ANALYSIS CENTER

T0097349

Current and Future Research on Labor Trafficking in the United States

JOE EYERMAN, MELISSA M. LABRIOLA, BELLA GONZÁLEZ

This research was published in 2023.

About This Report

Reducing the prevalence of all forms of human trafficking, including sex trafficking, labor trafficking, and child sexual exploitation, is a national priority that puts the U.S. Department of Homeland Security (DHS) in a prominent role. Given the scale, evolving "hidden" nature, and complexity of labor trafficking, combating the problem poses a significant challenge. The DHS Science and Technology Directorate (S&T) anti–human trafficking program is assessing the current state of and future needs for labor trafficking research in the United States. This effort will serve as a starting point for future social science–based S&T anti–human trafficking efforts focused on labor trafficking.

As part of this effort, DHS asked the Homeland Security Operational Analysis Center (HSOAC) to identify a scientifically sound research agenda—specifically, a list of research questions and research priorities—that would leverage existing U.S. and international efforts to address the growing phenomenon of labor trafficking. HSOAC experts developed a research agenda through an extensive review of the literature and meetings with experts from academia and nongovernmental organizations and with stakeholders from DHS and other parts of the U.S. government (expert interviews). The research agenda identified the barriers that needed to be addressed and the questions that needed to be answered to promote operationally relevant, focused, applied social and behavioral science research that would inform decision- and policymakers and assist operational partners in mitigating the crimes of labor trafficking and human trafficking more broadly.

This research was sponsored by S&T and conducted within the Infrastructure, Immigration, and Security Operations Program of the HSOAC federally funded research and development center (FFRDC).

About the Homeland Security Operational Analysis Center

The Homeland Security Act of 2002 (Section 305 of Public Law 107-296, as codified at 6 U.S.C. § 185) authorizes the Secretary of Homeland Security, acting through the Under Secretary for Science and Technology, to establish one or more FFRDCs to provide independent analysis of homeland security issues. The RAND Corporation operates HSOAC as an FFRDC for DHS under contract HSHQDC-16-D-00007.

The HSOAC FFRDC provides the government with independent and objective analyses and advice in core areas important to the department in support of policy development, decisionmaking, alternative approaches, and new ideas on issues of significance. The HSOAC FFRDC also works with and supports other federal, state, local, tribal, and public- and private-sector organizations that make up the homeland security enterprise. The HSOAC FFRDC's research is undertaken by mutual consent with DHS and is organized as a set of discrete tasks. This report presents the results of research and analysis conducted under task order 70RSAT21FR0000129, Current and Future Labor Trafficking Research in the United States.

The results presented in this report do not necessarily reflect official DHS opinion or policy.

For more information on HSOAC, see www.rand.org/hsoac. For more information on this publication, see www.rand.org/t/RRA1681-1.

Acknowledgments

This work benefited from the input and assistance of many people. We wish to thank our reviewers, Katya Migacheva of RAND and Dominique Roe-Sepowitz of Arizona State University, and Henry H. Willis of HSOAC for their feedback throughout this work. We also thank Nina Ryan and Francisco Walter for their assistance with overall production management and formatting, Anita Szafran for contributions to the literature search and reporting, and Lisa Bernard for reviewing and editing the report.

Summary

Reducing the prevalence of all forms of human trafficking, including sex trafficking, labor trafficking, and child sexual exploitation, is a national priority that puts the U.S. Department of Homeland Security (DHS) in a prominent role. Given the scale, evolving nature, and complexity of labor trafficking, combating the problem poses a significant challenge. The DHS Science and Technology Directorate (S&T) anti–human trafficking program is assessing the current state of and future needs for labor trafficking research in the United States. This effort will serve as a starting point for future social science–based S&T anti–human trafficking research and actions focused on labor trafficking.

As part of this effort, DHS asked the Homeland Security Operational Analysis Center (HSOAC) to identify a scientifically sound research agenda that would leverage existing U.S. and international efforts to address the growing phenomenon of labor trafficking. HSOAC experts developed a research agenda through an extensive review of the literature and meetings with experts from academia and nongovernmental organizations and with stakeholders from DHS and other parts of the U.S. government (expert interviews). The research agenda identified the barriers that would need to be addressed and the questions that would need to be answered to promote operationally relevant, focused, applied social and behavioral science research that would inform decision- and policymakers and assist operational partners in mitigating the crimes of labor trafficking and human trafficking more broadly.

Issue

DHS adopted the *Strategy to Combat Human Trafficking, the Importation of Goods Produced with Forced Labor, and Child Sexual Exploitation* (DHS, 2020) to guide its efforts to stop trafficking crimes. The strategy calls for DHS to "leverage all of our authorities in this fight . . . to end this urgent humanitarian issue" (DHS, 2020, p. iv). Specifically, in objective 2.1, the strategy calls for improved identification and reporting of suspected illicit activity, with DHS personnel supporting and coordinating with partners across the country (DHS, 2020, p. 12).

This objective aligns with the *S&T Strategic Plan 2021* (S&T, 2021) objective 1.2.2 to provide the best scientific knowledge in the context of DHS needs through closer relationships with the components and a better understanding of department needs (S&T, 2021, p. 15). This requires S&T to develop a research program that will result in a better understanding of the current state of DHS and other trafficking research, assess challenges with identifying potential victims, and develop methods for collaborating with partners.

Approach

DHS S&T human trafficking research supports the DHS and S&T strategic objectives through operationally relevant, end user–focused applied social and behavioral science research that enables decisionmakers, informs policymakers, and assists operational partners in mitigating the crime of labor trafficking. Given the scale, evolving nature, and complexity of labor trafficking, combating the problem poses a significant challenge.

In this exploratory study, we used qualitative methods to characterize the current state of U.S. and international labor trafficking research through a review of peer-reviewed and gray literature. The review also included DHS strategic and operational documents that describe DHS anti–labor trafficking objectives, programs, and component needs. We also identified and met with human trafficking experts from DHS, other federal agencies, HSOAC, nongovernmental organizations, survivor advocacy organizations, and academic institutions. The data collected through these sources were used to identify questions, study designs, and challenges for the research agenda. This effort focused exclusively on labor trafficking, an area that is underresearched and underidentified, especially domestically in the United States. This effort will serve as a starting point for future social science–based S&T anti–human trafficking efforts focused on labor trafficking.

Key Findings and Recommendations

We performed a literature review and a series of expert interviews to identify research questions in the literature and to prioritize those questions to align with DHS operational needs. We identified 18 research questions that should be addressed in the next six years; these eight are high-priority questions that DHS should address in the next 12 months:

- What risk factors influence migrants' high vulnerability to being forced into labor?
- How can the field of anti–labor trafficking be standardized (e.g., research, definitions, questionnaires, coding rules, evaluation design) in research and practice?
- How can federal, state, and local data systems be coordinated and organized to promote data-sharing, quantitative analysis, and rigorous evaluations?
- Who are the traffickers? What are their characteristics? How do they operate and communicate? How do they engage victims?
- How can stakeholders reduce undocumented workers' reluctance to participate in services? In programs? In research?
- What is the optimal protocol for labor trafficking investigations?
- How can decisionmakers identify evidence-based clinical screenings, identification, and training tools? What are best practices for identification, intervention, and investigation?
- What funding is needed to address labor trafficking research, investigations, and training?

Contents

Figures and Tables

Figures

Tables

CHAPTER ONE

Introduction

The Trafficking Victims Protection Act of 2000 (TVPA) (Pub. L. 106-386, 2000, Division A) defines *severe forms of trafficking in persons* as the "recruitment, harboring, transportation, provision, or obtaining of a person for labor or services, through the use of force, fraud or coercion for the purpose of subjection to involuntary servitude, peonage, debt bondage or slavery" (Pub. L. 106-386, 2000, § 103[8][b]). According to the U.S. Department of Health and Human Services, both bonded labor (in which labor is demanded as a means of repayment) and forced labor (in which a victim is forced to work against their will) are forms of labor trafficking. In a labor trafficking situation, violence, threats, lies, or other forms of coercion are used to force people to stay in exploitive work situations (Office on Trafficking in Persons, 2017). The International Labour Organization (ILO) estimates that 12.3 million people globally are victims of forced labor at any given time. The U.S. Department of State estimates that 14,500 to 17,500 people are trafficked into the United States each year, including both bonded and forced labor. Identifying labor trafficking victims is very difficult because

- they often are not aware of their rights
- they can be undocumented or displaced people who might not be well protected by current state and federal laws (e.g., they fear deportation if they come forward)
- there is no centralized reporting mechanism
- they can be undercounted because investigating and prosecuting labor trafficking cases can be very difficult.

Reducing the prevalence of all kinds of human trafficking, including sex trafficking, labor trafficking, and child sexual exploitation, is a national priority that puts the U.S. Department of Homeland Security (DHS) in a prominent role. Given the scale, evolving nature, and complexity of labor trafficking, combating the problem poses a significant challenge. The Homeland Security Operational Analysis Center (HSOAC), in partnership with the DHS Science and Technology Directorate (S&T) anti–human trafficking program, has assessed the current state of and future needs for labor trafficking research in the United States. This effort will serve as a starting point for future social science–based S&T anti–human trafficking efforts focused on labor trafficking.

In particular, DHS sought to identify a scientifically sound research agenda that could leverage existing U.S. and international efforts to address the growing phenomenon of labor trafficking. This agenda will advance operationally relevant, end user–focused applied social and behavioral science research that enables decisionmakers, informs policymakers, and assists operational partners in mitigating the crimes of labor trafficking and human trafficking more broadly.

The main goal of the project was to characterize the current state of U.S. and international labor trafficking research and identify research priorities. The following objectives guided the research:

- Identify key areas of research, publications, and findings about labor trafficking.
- Identify research that has been conducted but is not found in key publications.
- Understand the most-pressing topics related to labor trafficking research.
- Develop a research agenda.

To accomplish these objectives, a mixed-method exploratory study of the current state of labor trafficking research was conducted. The exploratory study consisted of a literature review and expert interviews that allowed researchers to document what is known in the field of labor trafficking research and, more importantly, what is not known. We organized what is not known into research questions. These research questions can serve as a starting point for future social science–based labor trafficking studies within S&T.

This study focused on labor trafficking in the United States and included a review of the U.S. and international literature and expert assessments of current U.S. and international programs. This study and the subsequent results focus solely on labor trafficking in United States, not sex trafficking or child sexual exploitation. The language and terms used in the field of labor trafficking can be nuanced, and, for the purposes of this report, we use the term *labor trafficking* in the broadest sense, which can include forced labor and labor exploitation. We understand that knowing the difference and distinguishing the indicators of labor trafficking from these other crimes is imperative as this research agenda moves forward.

CHAPTER TWO

Methods

To accomplish the objectives stated in Chapter One, we completed a thorough analysis of peer-reviewed and gray literature. The review also included DHS strategic and operational documents that describe DHS anti–labor trafficking objectives, programs, and component needs. We also met with and interviewed trafficking experts from DHS, other federal entities, HSOAC, nongovernmental organizations (NGOs), survivor advocacy organizations, and academic institutions. The data collected from these methods were used to identify questions, study designs, challenges, and data gaps for the research agenda.

All components of the project were approved by the RAND Corporation's institutional review board. The board's review includes the approval of data-sharing agreements and all data-collection methods, including written consent for qualitative procedures.

Data Collection

We conducted a literature review and a series of expert interviews to characterize the current state of labor trafficking research. The primary purpose of the literature review was to identify key topics and questions for the research agenda. We also used the literature review to inform the expert interview protocol. The expert interviews were used to validate and prioritize the topics and research questions from the literature review, identify additional research questions, and prioritize the research questions based on operational needs. See Figure 2.1.

FIGURE 2.1

Selection Process for Questions Included in the Research Agenda

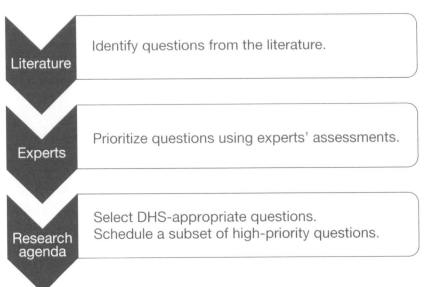

Literature Review

We conducted a systematic literature search using a strategy developed by a RAND librarian (see Appendix A for more about the search process). The strategy incorporated a series of search strings designed to query repositories of both academic and gray literature for recent publications about challenges and barriers to labor trafficking, both in the United States and abroad. The search strings were complemented by a series of inclusion and exclusion criteria delimiting the scope of the review. We screened retrieved hits by their titles and abstracts to identify articles that were out of scope (see exclusion reasons in Figure 2.2).[1] A uniform approach to screening was

---

[1] The exclusion process was intended to remove documents that were not research, not about trafficking, and not in line with the project objectives. The exclusion process also reduced the scope of the search to align with our limited project resources. We recognize that some exclusions (e.g., English only, no child studies) could reduce the coverage of the review.

FIGURE 2.2

Literature Selection Process

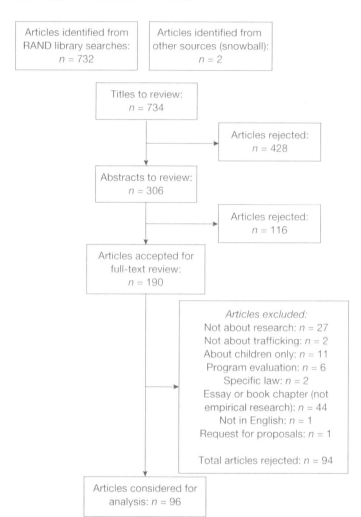

Articles identified from RAND library searches: *n* = 732

Articles identified from other sources (snowball): *n* = 2

Titles to review: *n* = 734

Articles rejected: *n* = 428

Abstracts to review: *n* = 306

Articles rejected: *n* = 116

Articles accepted for full-text review: *n* = 190

Articles excluded:
Not about research: *n* = 27
Not about trafficking: *n* = 2
About children only: *n* = 11
Program evaluation: *n* = 6
Specific law: *n* = 2
Essay or book chapter (not empirical research): *n* = 44
Not in English: *n* = 1
Request for proposals: *n* = 1

Total articles rejected: *n* = 94

Articles considered for analysis: *n* = 96

ensured by simultaneous screening of a subset of hits by multiple research-ers and subsequent consultations.

We supplemented the sources identified through our literature review with seminal works on relevant topics that were published prior to 2015 (ear-lier than our search period) where the seminal sources were needed in order to fully understand the state of current research. We also gathered sources on topics that were not covered in our literature review but that we knew from our own research and from expert input were important to discuss—these are identified as foundation issues and discussed in Chapter Four.

Figure 2.2 shows the selection process for the literature review. We started with 734 articles gathered from a RAND librarian and from supplemental sources. We began by conducting a review of the titles of the articles and removed 428 of the articles based on the relevance of the titles, leaving 306. Next, 116 of the articles were removed based on relevance of the abstracts, leaving 190 to be fully reviewed. Finally, 94 articles were removed, leaving 96 articles relevant to our study.

Expert Interviews

To accomplish the objective of providing a characterization of the current state of labor trafficking research, we also conducted interviews with experts. These interviews focused on specific research in which the individuals or their agencies were involved, what they thought were the most-pressing topics related to labor trafficking research, and what specific research needs were not being addressed by their agencies or the field. This approach ensured that we captured key areas of research or key publications and provided a nuanced perspective in our recommendations for research that might not have been drawn from the literature review alone.

The interviewees were drawn from experts at various government agencies working on labor trafficking, as well as researchers working in the education and nongovernment fields. The interviews were semistructured, following a unified topic guide (see Appendix B) but allowing for a discussion of unanticipated topics and lasted approximately one hour. Some of the interviews were conducted with multiple members of the same organization. In total, we conducted 12 interviews with 16 experts and three background meetings with teams involved in trafficking programming and research from the Department of State, Department of Justice, and DHS. Interviews were conducted by the team members, with one or two people leading the discussion and one person taking notes.

Analysis

Literature Review

The research team read the 96 articles, organized them into five topical categories, and extracted information by using a standardized data-extraction template in the form of a Microsoft Excel spreadsheet. Each row corresponded to a unique source, and each column corresponded to a line of inquiry to be answered by each source, such as the population studied, methods and data used, results, and most importantly, the research needs and questions identified by the authors. The five topical categories were

- 1: identification, investigation, and training
- 2: trafficking practices
- 3: methods and data gaps in the labor trafficking research field
- 4: victim experiences
- 5: roles of multinational organizations and partnerships.

Expert Interviews

Interview notes were coded following standard thematic analysis techniques (Boyatzis, 1998; Clarke, Braun, and Hayfield, 2015) to identify salient topics. Information was extracted about existing efforts in the anti–labor trafficking field and research or data gaps. Like in the process for the literature review, the notes were coded into topics. Table 2.1 indicates the seven topics identified and the number of times those topics were covered in the interviews.

It is important to note that five of the seven interview topics were also found in the literature review. It is those five topics around which we organized this report. This report synthesizes the results from our data collection in the five topical areas and develops a research agenda with suggested priority research questions and clear recommendations about how best to move the field forward. The two topics from the expert interviews that did not show up in the literature review—comparison to sex trafficking and policy implications—are discussed in the conclusion.

TABLE 2.1

Expert Interview Topics

Topic	Number of Times Discussed
Identification, investigation, and training	37
Methods and data	31
Trafficking practices	14
Partnerships	13
Victim experiences	9
Comparison to sex trafficking	9
Policy implications	6

Developing the Research Agenda

We combined the expert interviews with the literature review to identify the subset of research questions that were reported in both sources. We then prioritized the questions based on the urgency and operational relevance reported during our discussions with the experts. We also included questions that the experts considered important but were not identified in the literature review. These questions usually were specific to the mission or job requirements of the expert (e.g., specific data sources).

The prioritized list was further refined by including only those questions that met all of these criteria:

- aligned with the DHS mission
- were not part of ongoing or expected research by another federal entity or member of the academic research community
- could be implemented immediately (one year), in the near term (two to three years), or in the long term (four to six years).

CHAPTER THREE

Findings

Topic 1: Identification, Investigation, and Training

Results from the Literature Review

Some of the most-researched labor trafficking topics are the processes of identifying and screening for victims, properly intervening, investigating, enforcing cases, and training. Despite being the most-researched topics, they still have data and knowledge gaps, such as best practices for those processes that require further research. In this section, we explain what is known about these topics and what is left out of the literature and expert knowledge.

Screening and Identification

The literature indicates that certain characteristics, including demographics, create increased vulnerabilities for labor trafficking. Low socioeconomic status, prior victimization, homelessness, mental illness, age, involvement with the criminal justice system, limited education, gender, sexual orientation, and citizenship all contribute to one's likelihood of being trafficked (Dank et al., 2021; Schwarz et al., 2019). Additionally, some common indicators are used to identify possible labor trafficking cases. The United Nations Office on Drugs and Crime published "Human Trafficking Indicators," which outlines indicators for general trafficking and labor exploitation (Global Initiative to Fight Human Trafficking, undated). Also, the ILO published *ILO Indicators of Forced Labour* in 2012 (Special Action Programme to Combat Forced Labour, 2012), which outlines 11 indicators that law enforcement and other labor agencies can use as a guide to detect forced labor. There is also a federal definition of *labor trafficking* in the United States, created by the TVPA. All of this helped law enforcement and nongovernmental service agencies identify victims the same way (National Institute of Justice, 2016; Volodko, Cockbain, and Kleinberg, 2020).

Despite the fact that these indicators have been identified, large portions of the victim population are still going undetected. This is partially because the definitions describe human trafficking, labor exploitation, forced labor, and labor trafficking as overlapping actions. Although they are similar—specifically, because forced labor is a form of labor trafficking—they are not all the same. Also, some of the indicators of labor trafficking are outdated. The ILO indicators are based on the definition of *forced labor* decided on during the Convention Concerning Forced or Compulsory Labour, 1930 (commonly called the Forced Labour Convention) (Special Action Programme to Combat Forced Labour, 2012). This definition is outdated because recruitment methods, vulnerability factors, and indicators have changed tremendously since then. In addition, there is confusion about how many indicators are needed to signify that labor trafficking exists. Some indicators carry more weight than others, some can present themselves both in legal and illegal work, and some can affect different people differently. Scholars describe this as the continuum of vulnerability (Schwarz et al., 2019; Volodko, Cockbain, and Kleinberg, 2020), which explains people's levels of susceptibility to human trafficking based on their identities and experiences. Research on these indicators should take a holistic approach that considers how this continuum of vulnerability affect the ability to properly identify victims.

The literature also notes that the legal definition of *labor trafficking* is known to be ambiguous. Many scholars have said that one of the reasons it is so hard to identify victims and intervene is that the broad definition allows room for interpretation (Bales, Murphy, and Silverman, 2020; Beck et al., 2017; Farrell, Bright, et al., 2020; Farrell, Dank, et al., 2018). The specific words used in the ILO indicators of forced labor (see box), the TVPA, and individual state and country definitions all vary and, because of this, law enforcement and other anti–labor trafficking agencies have been found to have different ideas of what exactly defines *labor trafficking*, making proper identification of cases difficult.

ILO Indicators of Forced Labour

- Abuse of vulnerability
- Deception
- Restriction of movement
- Isolation
- Physical and sexual violence
- Intimidation and threats
- Retention of identity documents
- Withholding of wages
- Debt bondage
- Abusive working and living conditions
- Excessive overtime

Investigation

Labor trafficking investigations are relatively uncommon for a multitude of reasons. One main challenge is the overlap of labor trafficking with other crimes. Many service providers and law enforcement agencies report that it is hard to isolate labor trafficking offenses because they are usually categorized with some other crimes, such as sex trafficking or sex work (Dank et al., 2021; National Institute of Justice, 2016). For example, Farrell, Dank, and their colleagues found that, when any kind of human trafficking victims were identified, record systems did not acknowledge human trafficking as a form of victimization, leading officials to process and investigate the cases as other crimes (Farrell, Dank, et al., 2018). Narrowing this to just labor trafficking gets even more complicated with the overlap with sex trafficking. This leads to difficulty for officers trying to investigate labor trafficking as its own crime, as well as gaps in prevalence data. A lack of information-sharing also proves to inhibit labor trafficking investigations (Bracy, Lul, and Roe-Sepowitz, 2021). Partnerships between law enforcement, service agencies fighting labor trafficking, NGOs, and the public are important factors that seems to be missing in the research. Once a standardized definition and identification tool are developed, a uniform database should also be integrated into labor trafficking investigations to track data on potential victims and indicators of labor trafficking across all agencies and help them identify organizations and companies that are exhibiting exploitative behaviors (Farrell, Dank, et al., 2018). Furthermore, information-sharing will allow new technological methods to better estimate the number of victims and locate them. One example of such a method is multiple-system estimation, which has shown success in identifying the number of invisible victims (Farrell, Dank, et al., 2018). Research on how to transform this prevalence information into finding the actual victims should be prioritized.

Training

Law enforcement training typically teaches officers how to identify labor trafficking cases and correctly report them. These trainings generally frame labor trafficking as a foreign issue with non-U.S. victims and perpetrators (Dank et al., 2021). This framework ultimately affects success in identifying and investigating cases because more emphasis in actual work is placed on domestic criminal activity than on international crime. Additionally, gaps in existing literature show the need for best practices for training. Farrell, Dank, et al., 2018, acknowledges that one of the biggest challenges that law enforcement faces when trying to identify victims is an overall lack of law enforcement training. Clearly, the need for developing specialized training and curricula for law enforcement on identifying and investigating labor trafficking is a crucial need for future research (Dank et al., 2021; Doyle et al., 2019; Farrell, Dank, et al., 2018; National Institute of Justice, 2016). Ensuring that all officers are trained the same way will help close any remaining gaps in identification.

Finally, although most research focuses on how law enforcement and anti–labor trafficking service providers should be trained in identifying labor trafficking victims, another source of training has recently been included. Health care workers can interact with labor trafficking victims alone but are often unaware of how to identify them as victims or to properly intervene. Because of this, many scholars have emphasized the need to train health care workers (Beck et al., 2017; Mostajabian et al., 2019; Nordstrom, 2022), as well as psychiatric, legal, and social service workers (Beck et al., 2017; Nguyen et al., 2018). For example, Nordstrom found that educating health care providers on human trafficking increased knowledge about human trafficking and confidence in intervening. However, this knowledge decreased overtime, highlighting a need for ongoing education

(Nordstrom, 2022). Mostajabian and her colleagues also found that a specialized human trafficking training specifically for health care professionals was a more effective screening tool than general training for all service providers. This provides more evidence that a standardized, evidence-based assessment tool specific to labor trafficking should be researched and developed. This tool could be used universally among health care professionals and then extended to other kinds of providers.

Results from Interviews

Screening and Identification

The challenges of screening and identification of labor trafficking victims were topics brought up most by experts. Echoing the literature, many of them pointed out that, because labor trafficking often overlaps with other crimes, determining when a crime actually qualifies as labor trafficking is difficult. Because law enforcement and service agencies struggle with this, many people emphasized the need to improve techniques that look for labor trafficking victims at locations that have a higher vulnerability to trafficking. Specifically, one stakeholder noted, "DHS needs to work on screening on border and holding facilities." Developing better screening procedures in different agencies, such as U.S. Border Patrol, can help people not only identify victims and cases proactively but also understand labor trafficking patterns. Additionally, some experts suggested using previously solved labor trafficking cases to develop screening practices. Understanding the people involved in cases can help build clearer indicators of labor trafficking. This sentiment was supported by the literature reviews that surfaced the need to develop a standard definition and indicators of labor trafficking.

Investigation

Even with better screening protocols, problems exist with intervening in and investigating labor trafficking cases. One major barrier to labor trafficking investigations noted in the interviews was the lack of personnel, resources, and funding. Multiple experts noted that the agencies capable of conducting the investigations are too small and stretched too thin on other projects to fully investigate labor trafficking. Therefore, having a unit or person dedicated to labor trafficking could create internal agency pressure and be beneficial. Additionally, stakeholders noted that labor trafficking investigations are very labor-, time-, and resource-intensive. Often, this inhibits officials' ability to pursue a lead, especially when other crimes are easier and quicker to investigate. Because of this, research needs to be done on funding needs and promising practices to reduce the time and effort on labor trafficking cases so more can be investigated. Experts also noted that official and unofficial legal restrains limit the success of investigations. Some jurisdictions do not put pressure on labor trafficking cases because they are so resource-intensive, complicating efforts to bring these cases to prosecution.

Furthermore, many experts emphasized the lack of guidance and awareness about the process to investigate labor trafficking when cases are identified. With few successful example cases to follow and no official protocol for investigations, agencies struggle with data collection, where to refer cases, and how to take a victim-centered approach while conducting the investigation. A handbook that provides such information as the steps of the process, what evidence to collect, and examples of successful investigations is very important. One interviewee specifically noted, "There needs to be a better, more-specific, targeted training for everyone, not just HSI [Homeland Security Investigations]. All the agents live by their handbooks; it tells them how to run the investigations." Especially with rapid turnover of law enforcement, having an established knowledge base and protocol to follow is imperative.

Training

Finally, interviewees noted training needs. Frustrated with the current lack of protocols to follow, academics, NGOs, and DHS all identified the importance of developing best practices to train agents to screen for labor trafficking victims and intervene. Specifically, one stakeholder talked about the need to develop investigative training based on actual data instead of relying on workers' testimonies, which are not always reliable. Another mentioned developing training on preventive measures, such as recognizing patterns in confirmed cases to identify new cases. One example of this is a theory that, if multiple companies using the same employee recruitment methods have been confirmed to traffic workers, other companies using that recruitment method might also be linked to the trafficking. Even further, the interviews revealed the need for continued training. One interviewee noted, "There's resources and trainings available, but they've been one-and-done. We're sitting on good stuff, but it needs to be refreshed and out and frequent, given turnover in law enforcement and NGOs."

As discussed earlier, for each topic, a preliminary list of research questions on which DHS should focus have been identified. In Chapter Four, we prioritize the questions based on urgency.

Topic 1: Identification, Investigation, and Training Research Questions

- Does difficulty in identifying victims lead to labor trafficking being underreported?
- Can technology help with labor trafficking data-sharing?
- How can decisionmakers identify evidence-based clinical screenings, identification, and training tools? What are best practices for identification, intervention, and investigation?
- How much training is required to increase knowledge in both law enforcement and health care?
- How can agents in different components be prepared to intervene (e.g., the Transportation Security Administration, U.S. Customs and Border Protection)?
- Does monitoring victims of other trafficking crimes help identify labor trafficking victims?
- How can labor trafficking indicators better guide identification?
- How can stakeholders identify indicators of trafficking that do not come from worker testimony?
- Are the laws pertaining to labor trafficking difficult to enforce and prosecute?
- What is the best way to quickly build capacity so people are incentivized to work labor trafficking cases?
- How can investigations be proactive not reactive?
- What is the optimal protocol for labor trafficking investigations?
- What funding is needed to address labor trafficking research, investigations, and training?

- How do internal and external agency pressures shape the initiation and completion of investigations?
- How can the field of anti–labor trafficking be standardized (e.g., research, definitions, questionnaires, coding rules, evaluation design) in research and practice?

Topic 2: Trafficking Practices

Results from the Literature Review

Victims

Most research on victims focuses on what groups of people are most vulnerable to becoming victims. Factors that affect one's risk of being labor trafficked include economic and housing insecurity, lack of education, immigration status, gender, race and ethnicity, career, wages, and age (LeBaron, 2021; Nguyen et al., 2018; Paraskevas and Brookes, 2018; Schwarz et al., 2019). For example, the majority of research on labor trafficking victims focuses on how migrant workers are much likelier to be trafficked because of their living and working conditions. Many people who emigrate to another country for work often move with few resources and must rely on their employers for housing, wages, and food. As a result, they are unaware of their employee rights and become manipulated by their employers, which leads to low wages and poor working conditions in which the employee does not feel like they can step up for fear of losing their job or being deported (Ollus, 2016; Schwarz et al., 2019). Other data on victims show that vulnerability is not discrete. Schwarz et al., 2019, explains how different social factors create a continuum of vulnerability: Accumulating multiple risk factors makes one increasingly likely to become a victim. For this reason, identifying labor trafficking victims requires knowledge of a wide variety of social problems and inequities.

There are still significant data gaps for all these topics. Although clearly vulnerability factors for labor trafficking run on a continuum, identifying victims is still a challenge. Data gaps for specific groups create invisible victims whose voices are not heard. Men's voices, for example, are left out of some labor trafficking research because they are often more hesitant than others to report their experiences. Typical gender roles create an idea that men should be dominant and hold stable jobs to support their families. When they are trafficked and this does not occur, they can feel shameful and often do not report their victimhood, letting the labor trafficking continue (Shankley, 2021). Additionally, although migrant workers are known to be a vulnerable group, they too are hesitant to report their experiences out of fear of deportation. Thus, collecting data on their experiences, as well as those of other invisible victims, such as people experiencing homelessness, is integral to understanding the full scope of victims' experiences of labor trafficking.

Recruitment Methods

Studies on this topic focus on how perpetrators recruit victims, which differs based on media, outreach methods, and industry. Advances in technology have created new ways to manipulate and exploit workers. By utilizing online job platforms, employees lack a connection to their employers, which reduces their agency and increases the power imbalance, ultimately creating space for exploitation (Athreya, 2020). Other forms of recruitment include using fake immigration agencies to attract migrant workers, adopting young children to traffic, and traditional lying and manipulation (Hodge, 2019).

Despite having global indicators from the ILO, finding industries in which recruitment is high is still a struggle. Although Paraskevas and Brookes, 2018, shows that it is possible to map out the pathways that labor trafficking perpetrators take to recruit victims in the tourism industry, they also show that the industry workers' lack of awareness and training undermines these efforts to disrupt the process. Paraskevas and Brookes, 2018, shows the need for future research to map these pathways for other industries. It also highlights the need for data on how workers can be "guardians" by intervening in these pathways to disrupt the recruitment methods. Even further, more research on recruitment is especially needed pertaining to migrant workers. Migration brokers play an important role in labor trafficking. Migrants using brokers are often manipulated and exploited because they lack awareness of and accessibility to immigration options. Renshaw, 2016, highlights this gap in data on the role of migration brokers and shows the many ways in which exploitation is possible. More empirical data are needed on when and how the various migration pathways intersect with labor trafficking and how regulatory systems can be put into place to reduce this risk. Understanding these practices can help prevent labor trafficking by stopping activity before victims are recruited.

Industries

Research on this topic aims to investigate which industries foster labor trafficking practices more than others. One well-known industry that perpetuates labor trafficking is agriculture. The cotton and fishing fields both have histories of poor working conditions, low wages, and high demand that all foster exploitative and criminal labor practices. For example, a study on the fishing industry in New Zealand mapped out the labor trafficking that vessel workers experienced during all aspects of the job. With coercive recruitment methods, abusive working conditions, poor knowledge of employee rights, and exploitative practices while trying to exit the industry, these workers are being forced to comply with dangerous job demands (Stringer, Whittaker, and Simmons, 2016). Another industry that is vulnerable to labor trafficking practices is domestic work. Recent data show that homeworkers, such as caregivers or cleaners, are often not protected under antitrafficking laws and policies targeting large corporations, leaving these workers vulnerable (Ricard-Guay and Maroukis, 2017). Even when they are protected under laws and policies, domestic workers are typically unaware of their rights. Ultimately, the fields that have higher likelihoods of labor trafficking make up a large portion of the subjects of existing research.

Another part of literature on individual industries involves how companies sustain labor trafficking practices. Although there are policies meant to regulate labor trafficking in companies, these problems are still relevant. Stevenson and Cole, 2018, shows that, despite legislation in the United Kingdom that mandates disclosures about trafficking, many companies submit statements using methods similar to those they use for other social issues in supply chains instead of labor-specific policies. For example, some companies submit disclosures using methods for tracking sustainability measures instead of concerns specific to labor trafficking, such as the use of targeted code-of-conduct audits to third-party suppliers. Although most of this research focuses on legislation in European countries, it also recognizes the complex pathways of labor trafficking that involve multiple countries at once. Thus, developing a comprehensive and concise response to these global problems, which would need to include more-successful policies, is integral to overseeing company practices and ensuring legal work conditions everywhere (Davies, 2020). The consequences of enforcement, or lack thereof, also need to be analyzed in terms of this complex global pattern. Longitudinal studies are especially needed to track how companies' standards for reporting and regulation change over time (Amahazion, 2015).

Supply Chains

Perhaps one of the most-researched topics pertaining to labor trafficking practices today is supply chains. The globalization of goods has created transnational networks linking product suppliers, transporters, buyers, and consumers (Koekkoek, Marx, and Wouters, 2017; Carpenter, 2020; Lehr, 2020). When multiple companies and countries are involved in the production and distribution of products, it is harder to keep track of not only the origins and movements of the products (Lehr, 2020) but also labor rights violations in each step of the process (Koekkoek, Marx, and Wouters, 2017). Because of this problem, many governments have taken measures to increase accountability and transparency through regulatory policies. California's Transparency in Supply Chains Act (California Legislature, 2010), for example, prompts companies to create policies that address labor trafficking in their workforces (Koekkoek, Marx, and Wouters, 2017). Although measuring the effect that such policies have on decreasing labor trafficking, this act did make companies aware of the risks of noncompliance and prompted them to work toward more-positive practices. Traceability approaches have also been developed to increase knowledge about how and where products are sourced. Some of these technologies aid in identifying labor trafficking in smaller companies that are not as regulated (Lehr, 2020).

Results from Interviews

Regarding labor trafficking practices, the experts identified similar topics but more-specific data gaps and research needs than the literature review. The main topic discussed was recruitment methods. Experts acknowledged that research needs to focus on understanding the patterns of trafficking, such as who the traffickers are, how and where they operate, whether there is a foreign component, whether it is organized by a group or an individual, and how wages interact. To do this, multiple people recommended having a specific agency or unit collect cross-agency data and analyze patterns that emerge. Additionally, the experts emphasized the importance of Mexico's influence on labor trafficking in the United States. They agreed that labor trafficking processes, such as recruitment, use of proceeds, and crime patterns, need to be addressed on both sides of the border in order to really target the problems. Finally, like we found in the literature review, experts mentioned the importance of researching individual industries because labor trafficking practices can vary by field.

As discussed earlier, for each topic, a preliminary list of research questions on which DHS should focus have been identified. In Chapter Four, we prioritize the questions based on urgency.

Topic 2: Trafficking Practices Research Questions

- What are the industry-specific recruitment methods for labor trafficking? What are the nodes of intervention?
- When during the immigration process are people recruited? How many are trafficked in their home countries, en route to the United States, and in the United States?
- What is the role of the broker? How can it be investigated and researched?
- How has globalization influenced labor trafficking?
- How can disclosure policies increase accountability in companies?
- How can companies create internal policies that reduce labor trafficking while increasing efficiency?
- How can supply chain traceability technologies be used to reduce labor trafficking recruitment in supply chains?
- What trafficking is occurring in specific geographic areas? Who are the traffickers? What are their characteristics? How do they operate and communicate? How do they engage victims?
- What are the schemes and patterns of labor trafficking crimes? Are they systematic or opportunistic? Is there a foreign component? Is smuggling involved?
- How do traffickers modify their business models in response to changes in regulations and enforcement?

- How can stakeholders identify industry-specific patterns? What new technologies can help trace trafficking patterns and victims (e.g., isotope, microbiome, blockchain)?
- What risk factors influence migrants' high vulnerability to being forced into labor?

Topic 3: Methods and Data Gaps in the Labor Trafficking Research Field

Results from the Literature Review

Rigorous analysis of quality data is essential for evidence-based programming, focused interventions, improved victim services, increased prosecutions, and a better understanding of the causes and consequences of labor trafficking. The labor trafficking research field faces multiple method and data challenges that must be addressed before it can fully contribute to these objectives (Cockbain, Bowers, and Dimitrova, 2018). Quality measurement and analysis is more than an academic pursuit; it is crucial because it helps design evidence-based enforcement strategies and interventions (Pocock et al., 2020). These challenges are confounded by the complex nature of labor trafficking research, which includes measures of victim experiences, trafficker behaviors, case identification, prosecution, enabling industries and supply chains, immigration laws, and economic and social conditions at origin and destination. Many of these challenges are common to other multidisciplinary fields (Zhang and Cai, 2015) and include poor data quality, absence of standardization and common terminology, limited data availability, a field transitioning from primarily qualitative to quantitative and mixed-mode methods, and an absence of a clear authority for data and methods at the federal level.

Terminology, Standards, and Data Quality

The data-collection process begins with a research question and a clear understanding of the outcome measures. Although labor trafficking research questions often focus on how to reduce labor trafficking, there is not a clear definition of *labor trafficking* that is accepted as a field standard. This difficulty in measuring could contribute to underreporting (Goehrung,

2021), unclear or incomparable results across studies, and a limited ability to accumulate evidence to build a broader understanding of the problem (Zhang, 2012).

Terminology issues are confounded by the challenges and ethical issues inherent to studying vulnerable human subjects in challenging field conditions. These issues can result in missing data in both the identification and measurement of cases due to lack of victim cooperation, often caused by distrust of the government (U.S. Government Accountability Office [GAO], 2016), drug abuse resulting from trafficking, and difficulty in locating mobile potential victims (Cockbain, Bowers, and Dimitrova, 2018). In addition, the use of secondary data (e.g., hotlines, victim services, frontline medical monitoring) can put victims at risk of identity disclosure to traffickers and the public (Bales, Murphy, and Silverman, 2020). Finally, some population subgroups are difficult to identify. Groups who are often left out of victim data are men; migrant workers; youths who are sexual or gender minorities; and homeless youths.

Data Availability

An additional challenge for research is the limited availability of criminal court case data, victim experiences, and supply chain information. This is due in part to the absence of a clear federal authority for gathering and sharing labor trafficking case data thanks to overlapping jurisdictions (GAO, 2016), as indicated in Figure 3.1. An additional complexity is the central role that private industry plays in the labor trafficking process. Supply chain studies and studies of business models that support trafficking are difficult because the required data are mostly privately held by industry and might require new data for each business type, such as agriculture, mining, or fishing (Crane et al., 2022).

Transition from Qualitative to Quantitative and Analytic Tools

Much of the literature makes direct or passing reference to the importance of qualitative studies but also the need for more quantitative research and evaluations (Bryant and Landman, 2020). These studies include efforts to use statistical models to analyze the complex labor trafficking process, such as structural equation modeling, principal component analysis, and agent-based modeling (Majeed and Malik, 2017; McAlpine et al., 2021). Across

FIGURE 3.1

Federal Agencies Responsible for Investigating and Prosecuting Human Trafficking Crime

Investigative entities

Prosecutorial agencies

U.S. Department of Justice

U.S. Department of Justice

Federal Bureau of Investigation
Investigates a wide variety of violations of federal law, including allegations of sex and labor trafficking of adults and children in the United States

DHS

U.S. Immigration and Customs Enforcement HSI
Investigates cross-border criminal activity, including alleged sex and labor trafficking of adults and children in the United States

Offices of the U.S. Attorneys
Prosecute all types of federal crimes, including trafficking-related offenses, that fall within their jurisdictions

Criminal Section, Civil Rights Division

Human Trafficking Prosecution Unit
Prosecutes sex and labor trafficking of adults

U.S. Department of State

Bureau of Diplomatic Security
Investigates passport and visa fraud violations, which can be connected with crimes, such as trafficking

U.S. Department of Defense

Defense Criminal Investigative Service, U.S. Army Criminal Investigation Command, Naval Criminal Investigative Service, and Air Force Office of Special Investigations
Investigate alleged sex and labor trafficking involving service members, department contractors, and civilians; military police organizations investigate alleged sex work, which can be connected with human trafficking

Child Exploitation and Obscenity Section
Prosecutes federal child sexual exploitation offenses, including child sex trafficking, typically in partnership with the relevant U.S. Attorney's Office

U.S. Department of Labor

Inspector general
Investigates violations of federal law as related to department programs, which can be connected with crimes, such as trafficking

SOURCE: GAO, 2016, p. 9.

studies, we found the need for standardized data that can be analyzed with complex statistical models.

Results from Interviews

The experts echoed the concerns about data and methods identified in the literature. The greatest concern they voiced was with the accessibility of data. They observed that there was no DHS-wide data-sharing initiative that provided access to relevant information and verified that it was in a standard, clean, and usable format.[1] The experts said that they recognized the value and potential of data gathered by NGOs but highlighted the ethical challenges of using confidential requests for service or victim self-reports to meet analytic needs. They also noted that NGO data were generally collected as part of service delivery and often did not provide sufficient descriptive information for analysis. Experts also commented that, although NGO data can provide some of the information needed to develop programs and interventions, outside of the federal government, access to this data is limited. Most observed that the absence of a standardized database has prevented the generation of the accurate prevalence estimates that are required to understand the magnitude of the problem, show change following interventions, evaluate the benefits of pilots, and align appropriate resources to fund programs. One stakeholder commented that, because of these challenges, they were likelier to provide qualitative instead of quantitative data when asked to provide status updates on key labor trafficking issues.

The second most–important data analysis issue the experts voiced was poor data quality and limited verification. They noted that labor trafficking was underreported because many victims were reluctant to access social services or share their experiences because they feared arrest or deportation. They also commented that self-reported data were inaccurate because of response errors caused by contaminated field conditions (e.g., employer present during interviews), language barriers, and a lag between the labor trafficking experience and reporting. Finally, they noted that data gath-

---

[1] Like it is in other federal agencies, internal data-sharing across DHS is constrained by law enforcement and privacy sensitivities.

ered from case files often undercounted labor trafficking events because the investigations were more difficult and that investigators lacked effective training and resources needed to develop labor trafficking cases.

The experts also expressed a need for better data management tools and analytic models to access and process the labor trafficking data. Although the experts did not emphasize this need as much as the literature did, they did note that they needed a strong query tool that would allow them to access multiple data sources in different formats to build an event history for each victim that included the different stages of their labor trafficking experience.

As discussed earlier, for each topic, a preliminary list of research questions on which DHS should focus have been identified. In Chapter Four, we prioritize the questions based on urgency.

Topic 3: Methods and Data Gaps in the Labor Trafficking Research Field Research Questions

- How can federal, state, and local data systems be coordinated and organized to promote data-sharing, quantitative analysis, and rigorous evaluations?
- Where are the gaps in the current data systems, and what processes and resources are required to complete them?
- In investigations and data collection, how can stakeholders better identify victims who are more vulnerable to labor than sex trafficking (e.g., men, migrant workers, youths who are sexual or gender minorities, homeless youths)?
- How can stakeholders gather data to identify recruitment practices of traffickers?
- How should *labor trafficking* be defined for analysis, evaluation, and investigations? How can stakeholders develop a standard set of definitions for labor trafficking?
- How can training be developed and delivered to increase quality and standardization of data-collection efforts at the federal, state, local, and NGO levels?
- What are ethical challenges and risks of using secondary data for research about trafficking victims? How can these be mitigated?

- How can stakeholders access and analyze private-sector data to better understand the supply chains that benefit from forced labor?
- How can stakeholders analyze complex trafficking events, including recruitment, transport, brokering, and continued forced labor?
- What new technologies can help trace trafficking patterns (e.g., isotope, microbiome, blockchain)? What are the patterns?
- How can the data-collection process be standardized (e.g., definitions, questionnaires, coding rules, evaluation design) to produce comparable measures across studies?
- How can longitudinal studies inform the study of the effects that policy and regulatory interventions have on corporate supply chains and victim experience?
- What are the best analytic tools to use to examine trafficking, given the variability in quality, coverage, and definitions?
- What types of assessment tools will improve case identification by frontline workers in, for example, hospitals, border crossings, and law enforcement agencies?
- How can the academic research community be leveraged by policymakers to improve stakeholders' understanding and enforcement of trafficking?
- How can stakeholders measure recruitment practices for special populations?
- How can stakeholders identify and measure the characteristics and behaviors of traffickers?

Topic 4: Victim Experiences

Results from the Literature Review

As discussed in previous chapters, in terms of victim experience, the research has focused on what is known about identifying victims and certain risk factors that make some people more vulnerable to labor trafficking than others. What is lacking in the research is more information about the experiences of victims while being trafficked. Much of the research focuses on the experiences of foreign nationals who are either employed in the United States legally through a visa or illegally (Schwarz et al., 2019). The literature mentions that there is a misperception that labor trafficking is experienced differently for citizens of the United States because there is no threat to their citizenship, citizens have more rights, and citizens have the option to leave (Bihari, 2011; Dank et al., 2021). However, research has shown that, in fact, citizens face many barriers to exiting a job, including housing and food instability and fear of not being employable (Dank et al., 2021).

Finding the help necessary to seek legal action or even other viable employment options is often difficult and defeating. This often forces workers to stay in exploitative and abusive jobs because the alternatives might be even worse. Previous research indicates that victims of labor trafficking do not know where to go for help (Murphy, Doyle, and Murphy, 2020). One recommendation was to focus on increasing the availability and access to information about worker's rights. This could include making this information available in "businesses, local media outlets, social media, service providers, and other locations to increase awareness." Also, it is imperative that information be provided in multiple languages to ensure that everyone has access to the information. Other recommendations focused on reporting options, including making sure employees are aware of hotlines and anonymous reporting options for labor violations: Workers might also be skeptical that reporting will result in action (Norwood, 2020).

To effectively research the experiences of victims of labor trafficking, methods borrowed from research on vulnerable populations should be applied, such as a victim-centered and trauma-informed approach. A victim-centered approach works with the victims to actively participate in their situation and seeks to minimize additional trauma. A key aspect to this approach is to provide victims with services and resources.

Research should assess intervention strategies based on the role of the migration broker (Renshaw, 2016) to understand social networks; the roles of employers, crew leaders, and recruiters; and recruitment strategies (Azad, 2019). Also, it is imperative to understand trade unions' role in reducing migrant workers' vulnerability to labor trafficking (Marks and Olsen, 2015). More empirical data is needed on how these migration pathways intersect with labor trafficking and how regulatory systems can be put into place to reduce the risk of that happening.

Results from Interviews

On victim experiences, experts identified similar research needs as we did in the literature review. The main topic was how important victims' voices are when conducting research. Experts acknowledged that research needs to utilize a victim-centered approach, which would help gain trust from victims, which is imperative when collecting information on their experiences and gain knowledge about labor trafficking practices. This can help build victim knowledge, increase victims' reporting, and possibly increase reporting by others who might suspect labor trafficking. Researchers acknowledged the importance of victim voice while also acknowledging how difficult it is to know how to approach a situation. Interviewees also indicated that working with victims could be easier if more women were employed to communicate with and identify potential victims. Interviewees also mentioned the "hidden nature" of labor trafficking, including victims often being unaware of their rights and undocumented and displaced people being poorly protected by current state and federal laws and therefore less likely to report exploitive situations. There is no centralized reporting mechanism except for the national hotline, which might be inaccessible to the most at-risk population. The hidden nature of this population also makes successful investigations and prosecutions more difficult.

As discussed earlier, for each topic, a preliminary list of research questions on which DHS should focus have been identified. In Chapter Four, we prioritize the questions based on urgency.

Topic 4: Victim Experiences Research Questions

- Does awareness increase when stakeholders make education about workers' rights readily available in businesses, local media outlets, social media, service providers, and other locations?
- Does providing additional education and avenues to victims to report violations allow people to obtain assistance and report abusive situations more effectively?
- What do workers know about assessing agencies and brokers and about accessing services at destinations?
- What interventions and policies at both sources and destinations are designed to better address the challenges migrants face?

- How might employee representatives encourage corporate actions to reduce their trafficking practices when union rights are repressed?
- Is there a relationship between union activity and reduction of trafficking in corporations?
- How might consumers be better informed about labor trafficking?
- How does the work environment affect reporting? Do social networks increase self-reports? Are employers, crew leaders, and recruiters discouraging self-reports and therefore decreasing the accuracy of field studies?
- Who are the migration brokers? What types of interventions could prevent or reduce brokering?
- How and where do recruiters engage victims? What strategies do recruiters use? What interventions have been effective in countering recruiters?
- Can trade unions reduce migrant workers' vulnerability to trafficking?
- How can stakeholders increase workers' awareness of their rights? Which channels are most effective for communicating their rights?
- How can stakeholders reduce undocumented workers' reluctance to participate in services? In programs? In research?

Topic 5: The Roles of Multinational Organizations and Partnerships

Results from the Literature Review
Multinational Organizations

Because labor trafficking is so complex, much work and research are needed to understand companies' role in the perpetuation of human trafficking. This includes practices that are within businesses' control and scope to change, such as wages, sourcing practices, ethical supply chains, and adherence to labor laws and standards (Lehr, 2020). For example, multiple articles describe the need to understand business relationships and sourcing choices (Lloyd, Antonopoulos, and Papanicolaou, 2020). In particular, companies should clearly be able to document their sourcing choices. Researchers have assessed the Slavery and Trafficking Risk Template, a tool created to aid companies in collecting data from the supply chain and thus allows companies to make informed decisions (Carpenter, 2020).

In some instances, online petitioning and social media have been used to spread information and create pressure on corporations. Research is needed to fully understand whether those types of grassroots change movements are effective in both making companies change and changing consumers' minds.

The literature also points to companies beginning to draft trafficking statements (Koekkoek, Marx, and Wouters, 2017). One article indicates that research is needed on documenting how those statements evolve over time and the relationships between those statements and supply chain information disclosures.

Research is needed to fully understand the role of employers, crew leaders, and recruiters in the perpetuation of labor trafficking. The employer and company roles include wage reporting, working conditions, and the victim experience. Some industries that pay low wages and consistently report wage violations are likelier to be involved in labor trafficking. The wages and working conditions are not being regulated, analyzed, or properly enforced. As discussed in Chapter Two, workers reported that they often experienced violence, threats, and coercion by their employers.

Partnerships

The literature was also clear about the importance of the cooperation and communication between NGOs, companies, and the government. The government has a role in enforcement and creating transparency measures. However, it is difficult for governments to monitor whether goods entering the territory are free of labor rights abuses.

In addition, it is important to know companies' adherence to labor laws and reporting standards (Boucher, 2022). Government agencies should look beyond just economic violations to ensure that the full scope of interacting violations is considered when reporting or litigating these issues. Future research could consider the consequences of economic violations for countries engaged in labor trafficking.

Results from Interviews

The stakeholder interviews reiterated what we learned from the literature review—in particular, the importance of collaboration between agencies and NGOs in dismantling the legal barriers to prosecuting labor trafficking. One such collaboration mentioned was the cross-deputization of HSI and state and local officials. This type of collaboration between government agencies could facilitate an increase in the prosecution of labor traffickers. The interviewee said that the issue and problem are so great and cross multiple agencies that might not normally work together and that it is necessary to reshape the mentality about working together. This could include partnering with NGOs or immigration attorneys to access workers directly. An interviewee also indicated the role of foreign aid in incentivizing governments to strengthen their investigation and prosecution of cases.

As discussed earlier, for each topic, a preliminary list of research questions on which DHS should focus have been identified. In Chapter Four, we prioritize the questions based on urgency.

Topic 5: The Roles of Multinational Organizations and Partnerships Research Questions

- How helpful are initiatives and technologies for an effective traceability scheme?
- How can appropriate ethical supply chain tool kits be developed and introduced for business?
- How are organizations approaching legislatively mandated disclosure of information about labor trafficking? What legislative demands are present for entities in the United States?
- What do companies' public statements report about how they are detecting and remediating trafficking in their operations and supply chains?
- What mix of tools can governments use to address trafficking issues in large multinational and in small and medium-sized companies?
- What is the role of corporate self-regulation in changing behavior toward reduction and elimination of trafficking practices?
- What monitoring processes, such as auditing and inspection, will be necessary?

- What examples exist of successful and unsuccessful collaborations between NGOs and other nonprofits to reduce trafficking? (In what industries? What are the drivers of success?)
- What effects do online petitioning and social media have on public awareness and consumer behavior changes?
- How can international, federal, state, and local agencies investigate and research labor trafficking across multiple jurisdictions?

CHAPTER FOUR

Conclusion

Our review revealed significant knowledge gaps in several areas. In each of our five main focus areas—identification, investigation, and training; trafficking practices; methods and data gaps in the labor trafficking research field; victim experiences; and the role of multinational organizations and partnerships—we identified several priority research topics for which we believe better evidence will push the field forward and will contribute to reduced labor trafficking.

The List of Research Questions

Our primary goal was to identify high-priority research questions and create a research agenda to guide DHS S&T planning. We identified many research needs from the literature and the expert interviews. Specifically, we derived 18 research questions that could be addressed in one to six years. We ranked the 18 questions in the research agenda based on the urgency and the level of effort required to address the questions. We recommend that DHS consider these questions and encourage other federal entities or academia to pursue. Table 4.1 presents the questions.

Limitations

We used an inclusive approach for identifying research questions. We coded as a research question any stated research needs, topics, challenges, or questions identified in the literature review and the expert interviews. This resulted in a wide variety of research questions, some that were specific and

TABLE 4.1

Full List of Prioritized Research Questions

Implementation Period	Priority Rank	Question
Immediate (FY 2023)	1	What risk factors influence migrants' high vulnerability to being forced into labor?
	2	How can the field of anti–labor trafficking be standardized (e.g., research, definitions, questionnaires, coding rules, evaluation design) in research and practice?
	3	How can federal, state, and local data systems be coordinated and organized to promote data-sharing, quantitative analysis, and rigorous evaluations?
	4	Who are the traffickers? What are their characteristics? How do they operate and communicate? How do they engage victims?
	5	How can stakeholders reduce undocumented workers' reluctance to participate in services? In programs? In research?
	6	What is the optimal protocol for labor trafficking investigations?
	7	How can decisionmakers identify evidence-based clinical screenings, identification, and training tools? What are best practices for identification, intervention, and investigation?
	8	What funding is needed to address labor trafficking research, investigations, and training?
Near term (FYs 2024–2025)	9	How can stakeholders analyze a complex trafficking event, including recruitment, transport, brokering, and continued forced labor?
	10	How can training be developed and delivered to increase quality and standardization of data-collection efforts at the federal, state, local, and NGO levels?
	11	How do internal and external agency pressures shape the initiation and completion of investigations?
	12	What are ethical challenges and risks of using secondary data for research about trafficking victims? How can these be mitigated?

Table 4.1—Continued

Implementation Period	Priority Rank	Question
Long term (FYs 2026–2030)	13	How can international, federal, state, and local agencies investigate and research labor trafficking across multiple jurisdictions?
	14	What types of assessment tools will improve case identification by frontline workers in, for instance, hospitals, border crossings, and law enforcement agencies?
	15	How does the work environment affect reporting? Do social networks increase self-reports? Are employers, crew leaders, and recruiters discouraging self-reports and therefore decreasing the accuracy of field studies?
	16	How can stakeholders increase workers' awareness of their rights? Which channels are most effective for communicating their rights?
	17	What new technologies can help trace trafficking patterns (e.g., isotope, microbiome, blockchain)? What are the patterns?
	18	What are industry-specific recruitment methods for labor trafficking? What are the nodes of intervention?

NOTE: FY = fiscal year.

others that were very general. We do not expect all of them to be ready to map to a specific research study, nor do we provide specific research methods, funding estimates, or amounts of time needed to conduct the research; instead, we expect that research questions identified in this agenda will be used to guide resource allocation and research design conversations.

A few limitations of the study should be discussed. Because of resource constraints, the literature review could include only articles written in English; we were able to interview only a small sample of experts; and we had to limit our literature search to 2015 to the time of our research. In addition, because of the scope of the work, we were limited to focusing only on labor trafficking; although we were able to look at labor trafficking broadly, we were not able to focus on sex trafficking or child exploitation. We acknowledge that, by excluding this additional research, methods and findings from that work could contribute to the labor trafficking field. This work was conducted for DHS, so our scope was limited, with our understanding that additional work would be better situated to be conducted by adjacent agencies.

Interviewees brought up additional topics that, although they were not main research needs, still hold value for increasing knowledge about labor trafficking:

- First, experts emphasized the comparison between labor trafficking and sex trafficking. Because much less is known about labor trafficking practices and patterns than about those for sex trafficking, labor trafficking investigations are much more resource- and time-intensive. Additionally, when labor trafficking cases are identified, they are much less likely to be fully investigated and prosecuted. Although the comparison of sex and labor trafficking was not posed as a topic in the research agenda, this barrier is important to acknowledge when dealing with labor trafficking investigations.
- Another topic identified in the stakeholder interviews was policy implications. Although it was discussed only briefly, the experts noted how policy implications are bidirectional. Policy needs to be translated to operational actions, and what is known to work operationally needs to inform policy. Although similar policy recommendations, especially about supply chains, were brought up in the literature reviews, this topic was less relevant to the research agenda and thus was not analyzed as much as the others.

Recommendations

Our primary objective was to identify high-priority research questions and create a research agenda to guide DHS S&T planning. We identified many research needs from the literature and many operationally relevant needs from the expert interviews. We selected 18 research questions that could be addressed in one to six years. We then ranked the 18 questions in the research agenda based on the urgency and the level of effort required to address the questions and selected eight most-immediate questions. We recommend that DHS S&T take immediate action over the next 12 months to study those eight immediate questions.

This report presents an overview of labor trafficking research, where the gaps are, and where research can significantly improve the state of the field. The ultimate goal of this project was to present a research agenda, with the goal of identifying areas in which producing new, rigorous evidence could have the largest impact on labor trafficking. Our research agenda is aimed at DHS, policymakers, researchers, and practitioners, whose participation in any solution is essential. Ultimately, the suggestions that come out of improved research in this area should address labor trafficking issues, reduce victimization, and increase investigation and prosecution.

The Literature Review Search Process

We conducted a systematic literature search using a strategy developed by a RAND librarian. The strategy incorporated a series of search strings designed to query repositories of both academic and gray literature for recent publications about challenges in and barriers of anti–labor trafficking efforts, both in the United States and abroad. The search strings were complemented by a series of inclusion and exclusion criteria delimiting the scope of the review.

We searched the following databases:

- Academic Search Complete
- Business Source Complete
- Criminal Justice Abstracts
- Index to Legal Periodicals
- National Criminal Justice Reference Services Abstracts
- Public Affairs Information Service
- Policy File Index
- Scopus
- Social Sciences Abstracts
- Sociological Abstracts
- Web of Science.

In the three searches, we limited our search terms as follows:

- Each search string was limited to the title, abstract, or subject fields.
- We excluded any source not in English.

- We excluded all newspaper sources.
- We excluded any item published before 2015.
- We made no exclusions based on country of origin (we included both U.S. and non-U.S. sources).

Table A.1 shows the criteria that varied between the three searches, including the search string used in each search.

TABLE A.1
Search Terms and Criteria

Criterion	Search A: Knowledge Gaps	Search B: Agency Practices	Search C: Existing Evidence
Include dissertations, theses, and magazine sources.	x	x	
Include nonempirical sources.	x	x	
Unless an item describes an actual executed policy change or adoption, include only those recommendations coming from a recognized authority.		x	
Place no a priori limitations on the methodology of the source.			x
Search string	("labour traffick*" OR "labor traffick*" OR "modern slave*" OR "forced labor*" OR "forced labour*" OR "slave labor*" OR "slave labour*") AND (gap OR miss* OR know* OR need OR requir*) AND (evidence OR data OR information OR proof OR knowledge OR "research agenda")	("labour traffick*" OR "labor traffick*" OR "modern slave*" OR "forced labor*" OR "forced labour*" OR "slave labor*" OR "slave labour*") AND (reduc* OR avoid* OR prevent* OR mitigat* OR address* OR tackl* OR resolv* OR investigat* OR minimiz* OR punish* OR prosecut* OR remed* OR restor*) AND (policy OR policies OR program* OR interven* OR practice OR initiative OR "research agenda")	("labour traffick*" OR "labor traffick*" OR "modern slave*" OR "forced labor*" OR "forced labour*" OR "slave labor*" OR "slave labour*") AND (reduc* OR avoid* OR prevent* OR mitigat* OR address* OR tackl* OR resolve* OR investigat* OR minimiz* OR punish* OR prosecut* OR remed* OR restor*) AND (policy OR policies OR program* OR interven* OR practice OR initiative OR "research agenda")

Questions for the Expert Interviews

The interviews were semistructured, following a unified topic guide. These questions were used as a guide and adapted for each person and agency.

Questions for Expert Interviews

- How does your agency (organization) address trafficking, or how does countertrafficking fit into your agency mission?
  - Does your agency include both [anti–]labor [trafficking] and [anti–] sex trafficking activities?
  - Does your agency have staff dedicated to countertrafficking?
  - Is there a report or other documentation we should read?
- Where does your agency encounter trafficking? Immigrants at the border? Importation of trafficked goods? Other?
  - What are the most-common types of labor trafficking you encounter?
- Do you have research questions about labor trafficking, such as measuring program effectiveness, training requirements, or prevalence?
  - Do you have a research program that addresses those questions?
  - What are your greatest research needs?
  - Which research projects are highest priority?
  - How are the research priorities developed?
  - Are your priorities country specific, topic specific, methods focused, or other?
  - What barriers do you encounter when conducting research?
  - How are the research programs funded?

- – How is the research implemented? Through your agency, the centers of excellence, DHS S&T, or other?
- – Who are the consumers of your research? How do they contribute to the research process?
- – Are there research needs that are not addressed by your program or the field (e.g., methods studies, victim identification, measuring unseen population, identifying forced labor goods)? Why?
- Do you partner with the private sector in your research or programs?
- What are the most at-risk industries for labor trafficking?
- What are the specific vulnerabilities of labor trafficking victims (do they differ from sex trafficking victims)?
- How do you address the intersection of international and U.S. domestic labor trafficking?
- Are there other experts in your organization or the broader field whom we should contact?

Abbreviations

DHS	U.S. Department of Homeland Security
FY	fiscal year
HSI	Homeland Security Investigations
HSOAC	Homeland Security Operational Analysis Center
ILO	International Labour Organization
NGO	nongovernmental organization
S&T	Science and Technology Directorate
TVPA	Trafficking Victims Protection Act of 2000

References

Amahazion, FikreJesus, "Human Trafficking: The Need for Human Rights and Government Effectiveness in Enforcing Anti-Trafficking," *Global Crime*, Vol. 16, No. 3, 2015.

Athreya, Bama, "Slaves to Technology: Worker Control in the Surveillance Economy," *Anti-Trafficking Review*, No. 15, September 2020.

Azad, Ashraful, "Recruitment of Migrant Workers in Bangladesh: Elements of Human Trafficking for Labor Exploitation," *Journal of Human Trafficking*, Vol. 5, No. 2, 2019.

Bales, Kevin, Laura T. Murphy, and Bernard W. Silverman, "How Many Trafficked People Are There in Greater New Orleans? Lessons in Measurement," *Journal of Human Trafficking*, Vol. 6, No. 4, 2020.

Beck, Dana C., Kristen R. Choi, Michelle L. Munro-Kramer, and Jody R. Lori, "Human Trafficking in Ethiopia: A Scoping Review to Identify Gaps in Service Delivery, Research, and Policy," *Trauma, Violence, and Abuse*, Vol. 18, No. 5, December 2017.

Bihari, Luiz Arthur, "Clashing Laws: Exploring the Employment Rights of Undocumented Migrants," *University of Toronto Faculty of Law Review*, Vol. 69, No. 2, Spring 2011.

Boucher, Anna, "'What Is Exploitation and Workplace Abuse?' A Classification Schema to Understand Exploitative Workplace Behaviour Towards Migrant Workers," *New Political Economy*, Vol. 27, No. 4, 2022.

Boyatzis, Richard E., *Transforming Qualitative Information: Thematic Analysis and Code Development*, Thousand Oaks, Calif.: Sage Publications, 1998.

Bracy, Kristen, Bandak Lul, and Dominique Roe-Sepowitz, "A Four-Year Analysis of Labor Trafficking Cases in the United States: Exploring Characteristics and Labor Trafficking Patterns," *Journal of Human Trafficking*, Vol. 7, No. 1, 2021.

Bryant, Katharine, and Todd Landman, "Combatting Human Trafficking Since Palermo: What Do We Know About What Works?" *Journal of Human Trafficking*, Vol. 6, No. 2, 2020.

California Legislature, Transparency in Supply Chains Act, Senate Bill 657, September 30, 2010.

Carpenter, Sarah, "Developing Effective Programmes to Protect Modern Corporate Supply Chains Against Human Trafficking and Slavery," *Journal of Supply Chain Management, Logistics and Procurement*, Vol. 2, No. 3, Spring 2020.

Clarke, Victoria, Virginia Braun, and Nikki Hayfield, "Thematic Analysis," in Jonathan A. Smith, ed., *Qualitative Psychology: A Practical Guide to Research Methods*, London: SAGE Publications, 2015.

Cockbain, Ella, Kate Bowers, and Galina Dimitrova, "Human Trafficking for Labour Exploitation: The Results of a Two-Phase Systematic Review Mapping the European Evidence Base and Synthesising Key Scientific Research Evidence," *Journal of Experimental Criminology*, Vol. 14, September 2018.

Convention Concerning Forced or Compulsory Labour, Alb.–Alg.–Angl.–Ant. & Barb.–Arg.–Arm.–Austl.–Austria–Azer.–Bah.–Bahr.–Bangl.–Barb.–Belr.–Belg.–Belize–Benin–Plurinational State of Bol.–Bosn. & Herz.–Bots.–Braz.–Bulg.–Burk. Faso–Burundi–Cabo Verde–Cambodia–Cameroon–Can.–Cent. Afr. Rep.–Chad–Chile–China–Colom.–Comoros–Congo–Cook Islands–Costa Rica–Côte d'Ivoire–Croat.–Cuba–Cyprus–Czech–Dem. Rep. Congo–Den.–Djib.–Dominica–Dom. Rep.–Ecuador–Egypt–El Sal.–Eq. Guinea–Eri.–Est.–Eswatini–Eth.–Fiji–Fin.–Fr.–Gabon–Gam.–Geor.–Ger.–Ghana–Greece–Gren.–Guat.–Guinea–Guinea-Bissau–Guy.–Haiti–Hond.–Hung.–Ice.–India–Indon.–Islamic Republic of Iran–Iraq–Ir.–Isr.–It.–Jam.–Japan–Jordan–Kaz.–Kenya–Kiribati–Kuwait–Kyrg.–Lao People's Democratic Republic–Lat.–Leb.–Lesotho–Liber.–Libya–Lith.–Lux.–Madag.–Malawi–Malay.–Maldives–Mali–Malta–Mauritania–Mauritius–Mex.–Mong.–Montenegro–Morocco–Mozam.–Myan.–Namib.–Nepal–Neth.–N.Z.–Nicar.–Niger–Nigeria–N. Maced.–Nor.–Oman–Pak.–Pan.–Papua N.G.–Para.–Peru–Phil.–Pol.–Port.–Qatar–Republic of Kor.–Republic of Mold.–Rom.–Russian Federation–Rwanda–St. Kitts & Nevis–St. Lucia–St. Vincent–Samoa–San Marino–São Tomé & Principe–Saudi Arabia–Sen.–Serb.–Sey.–Sierra Leone–Sing.–Slovk.–Slovn.–Solom. Is.–Som.–S. Afr.–South Sudan–Spain–Sri Lanka–Sudan–Surin.–Swed.–Switz.–Syrian Arab Republic–Taj.–Thai.–Timor-Leste–Togo–Trin. & Tobago–Tunis.–Turkm.–Türkiye–Uganda–Ukr.–U.A.E.–U.K. of Gr. Brit. and N. Ir.–United Republic of Tanz.–Uru.–Uzb.–Vanuatu–Bolivarian Republic of Venez.–Viet.–Yemen–Zam.–Zim., June 28, 1930, 39 U.N.T.S. 55.

Crane, Andrew, Genevieve LeBaron, Kam Phung, Laya Behbahani, and Jean Allain, "Confronting the Business Models of Modern Slavery," *Journal of Management Inquiry*, Vol. 31, No. 3, July 2022.

Dank, Meredith, Amy Farrell, Sheldon Zhang, Andrea Hughes, Stephen Abeyta, Irina Fanarraga, Cameron P. Burke, and Veyli Ortiz Solis, *An Exploratory Study of Labor Trafficking Among U.S. Citizen Victims*, final research report, John Jay College of Criminal Justice, Northeastern University, University of Massachusetts, report for the National Institute of Justice, September 2021.

Davies, Jon, "Criminological Reflections on the Regulation and Governance of Labour Exploitation," *Trends in Organized Crime*, Vol. 23, March 2020.

DHS—*See* U.S. Department of Homeland Security.

Doyle, David M., Clíodhna Murphy, Muiread Murphy, Pablo Rojas Coppari, and Rachel J. Wechsler, "'I Felt Like She Owns Me': Exploitation and Uncertainty in the Lives of Labour Trafficking Victims in Ireland," *British Journal of Criminology*, Vol. 59, No. 1, January 2019.

Farrell, Amy, Katherine Bright, Ieke de Vries, Rebecca Pfeffer, and Meredith Dank, "Policing Labor Trafficking in the United States," *Trends in Organized Crime*, Vol. 23, March 2020.

Farrell, Amy, Meredith Dank, Matthew Kafafian, Sarah Lockwood, Rebecca Pfeffer, Andrea Hughes, and Kyle Vincent, *Capturing Human Trafficking Victimization Through Crime Reporting*, report for the National Institute of Justice, January 2018.

GAO—*See* U.S. Government Accountability Office.

Global Initiative to Fight Human Trafficking, Office on Drugs and Crime, United Nations, "Human Trafficking Indicators," undated.

Goehrung, Ryan, "Evaluating the Criminal Justice Approach to Human Trafficking in Taiwan," *Journal of Human Trafficking*, Vol. 7, No. 1, 2021.

Hodge, David R., "Internationally Trafficked Men in the USA: Experiences and Recommendations for Mental Health Professionals," *British Journal of Social Work*, Vol. 49, No. 3, April 2019.

Koekkoek, Marieke, Axel Marx, and Jan Wouters, "Monitoring Forced Labour and Slavery in Global Supply Chains: The Case of the California Act on Transparency in Supply Chains," *Global Policy*, Vol. 8, No. 4, November 2017.

LeBaron, Genevieve, "Wages: An Overlooked Dimension of Business and Human Rights in Global Supply Chains," *Business and Human Rights Journal*, Vol. 6, No. 1, 2021.

Lehr, Amy K., *New Approaches to Supply Chain Traceability: Implications for Xinjiang and Beyond*, Washington, D.C.: Center for Strategic and International Studies, November 16, 2020.

Lloyd, Anthony, Georgios A. Antonopoulos, and Georgios Papanicolaou, "'Illegal Labour Practices, Trafficking and Exploitation': An Introduction to the Special Issue," *Trends in Organized Crime*, Vol. 23, March 2020.

Majeed, Muhammad Tariq, and Amna Malik, "Selling Souls: An Empirical Analysis of Human Trafficking and Globalization," *Pakistan Journal of Commerce and Social Sciences*, Vol. 11, No. 1, April 30, 2017.

Marks, Eliza, and Anna Olsen, "The Role of Trade Unions in Reducing Migrant Workers' Vulnerability to Forced Labour and Human Trafficking in the Greater Mekong Subregion," *Anti-Trafficking Review*, No. 5, September 2015.

McAlpine, Alys, Ligia Kiss, Cathy Zimmerman, and Zaid Chalabi, "Agent-Based Modeling for Migration and Modern Slavery Research: A Systematic Review," *Journal of Computational Social Science*, Vol. 4, May 2021.

Mostajabian, Salina, Diane Santa Maria, Constance Wiemann, Elizabeth Newlin, and Claire Bocchini, "Identifying Sexual and Labor Exploitation Among Sheltered Youth Experiencing Homelessness: A Comparison of Screening Methods," *International Journal of Environmental Research and Public Health*, Vol. 16, No. 3, February 2019.

Murphy, Clíodhna, David M. Doyle, and Muiréad Murphy, "'Still Waiting' for Justice: Migrant Workers' Perspectives on Labour Exploitation in Ireland," *Industrial Law Journal*, Vol. 49, No. 3, September 2020.

National Institute of Justice, *How Does Labor Trafficking Occur in U.S. Communities and What Becomes of the Victims?* August 31, 2016.

Nguyen, Phuong T., Joanna Lamkin, John H. Coverdale, Samuel Scott, Karen Li, and Mollie R. Gordon, "Identifying Human Trafficking Victims on a Psychiatry Inpatient Service: A Case Series," *Psychiatric Quarterly*, Vol. 89, No. 2, June 2018.

Nordstrom, B. M., "Multidisciplinary Human Trafficking Education: Inpatient and Outpatient Healthcare Settings," *Journal of Human Trafficking*, Vol. 8, No. 2, 2022.

Norwood, Jeremy S., "Labor Exploitation of Migrant Farmworkers: Risks for Human Trafficking," *Journal of Human Trafficking*, Vol. 6, No. 2, 2020.

Office on Trafficking in Persons, Administration for Children and Families, U.S. Department of Health and Human Services, "Fact Sheet: Human Trafficking," OTIP-FS-18-01, November 21, 2017.

Ollus, Natalia, "Forced Flexibility and Exploitation: Experiences of Migrant Workers in the Cleaning Industry," *Nordic Journal of Working Life Studies*, Vol. 6, No. 1, 2016.

Paraskevas, Alexandros, and Maureen Brookes, "Nodes, Guardians and Signs: Raising Barriers to Human Trafficking in the Tourism Industry," *Tourism Management*, Vol. 67, August 2018.

Pocock, Nicola Suyin, Ligia Kiss, Mamata Dash, Joelle Mak, and Cathy Zimmerman, "Challenges to Pre-Migration Interventions to Prevent Human Trafficking: Results from a Before-and-After Learning Assessment of Training for Prospective Female Migrants in Odisha, India," *PLoS ONE*, Vol. 15, No. 9, 2020.

Public Law 106-386, Victims of Trafficking and Violence Protection Act of 2000, October 28, 2000.

Public Law 107-296, Homeland Security Act of 2002, November 25, 2002.

Renshaw, Lauren, "Migrating for Work and Study: The Role of the Migration Broker in Facilitating Workplace Exploitation, Human Trafficking and Slavery," *Trends and Issues in Crime and Criminal Justice*, No. 527, December 2016.

Ricard-Guay, Alexandra, and Thanos Maroukis, "Human Trafficking in Domestic Work in the EU: A Special Case or a Learning Ground for the Anti-Trafficking Field?" *Journal of Immigrant and Refugee Studies*, Vol. 15, No. 2, 2017.

Schwarz, Corinne, Daniel Alvord, Dorothy Daley, Megha Ramaswamy, Emily Rauscher, and Hannah Britton, "The Trafficking Continuum: Service Providers' Perspectives on Vulnerability, Exploitation, and Trafficking," *Affilia*, Vol. 34, No. 1, February 2019.

Science and Technology Directorate, U.S. Department of Homeland Security, *S&T Strategic Plan 2021*, January 25, 2021.

Shankley, William, "Gender, Modern Slavery and Labour Exploitation: Experiences of Male Polish Migrants in England," *Journal of Ethnic and Migration Studies*, 2021.

Special Action Programme to Combat Forced Labour, International Labour Organization, *ILO Indicators of Forced Labour*, October 1, 2012.

S&T—*See* Science and Technology Directorate.

Stevenson, Mark, and Rosanna Cole, "Modern Slavery in Supply Chains: A Secondary Data Analysis of Detection, Remediation and Disclosure," *Supply Chain Management*, Vol. 12, No. 3, 2018.

Stringer, Christina, D. Hugh Whittaker, and Glenn Simmons, "New Zealand's Turbulent Waters: The Use of Forced Labour in the Fishing Industry," *Global Networks*, Vol. 16, No. 1, January 2016.

U.S. Code, Title 6, Domestic Security; Chapter 1, Homeland Security Organization; Subchapter III, Science and Technology in Support of Homeland Security; Section 185, Federally Funded Research and Development Centers.

U.S. Department of Homeland Security, *Strategy to Combat Human Trafficking, the Importation of Goods Produced with Forced Labor, and Child Sexual Exploitation*, January 2020.

U.S. Government Accountability Office, *Human Trafficking: Agencies Have Taken Steps to Assess Prevalence, Address Victim Issues, and Avoid Grant Duplication*, Washington, D.C., GAO-16-555, June 28, 2016.

Volodko, Ada, Ella Cockbain, and Bennett Kleinberg, "'Spotting the Signs' of Trafficking Recruitment Online: Exploring the Characteristics of Advertisements Targeted at Migrant Job-Seekers," *Trends in Organized Crime*, Vol. 23, March 2020.

Zhang, Sheldon X., *Trafficking of Migrant Laborers in San Diego County: Looking for a Hidden Population*, San Diego, Calif.: San Diego State University, final report submitted to the National Institute of Justice, U.S. Department of Justice, 2012.

Zhang, Sheldon X., and Li Cai, "Counting Labour Trafficking Activities: An Empirical Attempt at Standardized Measurement," in Kristiina Kangaspunta, ed., *Forum on Crime and Society*, Vol. 8, 2015.